LET'S GO TO THE LITURGY

What do you do?

St Shenouda Press

8419 Putty Rd, Putty, NSW 2330
Sydney, Australia

www.stshenoudapress.com

ISBN 13: 978-1-7638415-3-6

SHENOUDA PRESS

AGPIA

We go to Church and use the Agpia to pray.

Every hour has meaning, it's how we start the day.

Agpia reminds me what Jesus did for me.

He gave His life for us, we recall joyfully.

OFFERTORY

Abouna signs the cross, and chooses the Holy Bread.

He prays on it, and raises it above his head.

He picks the most perfect one, looking with much care.

We bow and worship, "Lord have mercy" is our prayer.

LITURGY OF THE WORD

Deacons read the chosen passages of the day.

The words shine in our hearts, they pave for us the way.

We listen carefully, and see what we can learn.

The words of Christ we hear, to Him our hearts do turn.

PRAYER OF RECONCILIATION

Abouna tells the story, we fell from Paradise,

Then Jesus saved us, with His blood He paid the price.

Now we're friends with God, and also friends with each other,

We exchange a holy kiss: the Church is our mother.

ANAPHORA

Here we all remember that Heaven is our end,

Abouna describes it, and deacon says "let us attend".

We close our eyes and feel, we are in Heaven too,

We worship and tell God, all glory is due to You.

INSTITUTION NARRATIVE

The Holy Spirit now comes down, a mystery so divine,

He turns the bread into Christ's Body, and His Blood from wine.

Jesus taught us how to break bread, the disciples were with Him.

That's why we say, "We believe, confess and glorify Him".

SHORT LITANIES

Then we pray for seven things, the Church and his Holiness the Pope.

We pray for all the bishops and priests, who guide us and give us hope.

We pray for the deacons and servants, so that they may endure.

We pray for the Earth God has given us, and the sick He may cure.

COMMEMORATION
OF SAINTS

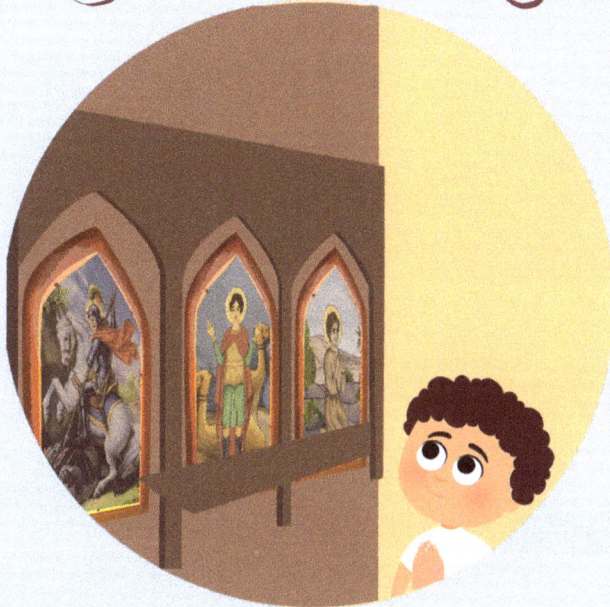

Here we remember the holy saints, who lived for the Lord.

We pray that they may be with us, they are loved and adored.

We see their icons around the church, they are with us today.

We ask that God gives us the strength, to love, preach and pray.

THE FRACTION

Abouna breaks the body into separate pieces, then

He reads a special prayer relating to the season.

We prepare to respond, and listen very carefully.

We can say "kerya-layson", or "Lord have mercy".

COMMUNION

Abouna confesses the bread is Jesus' Holy Body,

And the wine mixed with water, is the Blood He shed for me.

We take off our shoes, girls and ladies cover their hair,

We wait in line, and receive Communion with care.

DISMISSAL

After Holy Communion, Abouna sprays us with the water.

We love our Coptic Church, we are her sons and daughters.

More blessing is at the door in the form of 'baraka' bread.

We are united as the body, and Christ is our Head.

www.ingramcontent.com/pod-product-compliance
Lightning Source LLC
Chambersburg PA
CBHW050257090426
42734CB00022B/3485